MAGIC JOHNSON

HERO ON AND OFF COURT

BY BILL GUTMAN

MILLBROOK SPORTS WORLD

THE MILLBROOK PRESS

BROOKFIELD, CONNECTICUT

Published by The Millbrook Press
2 Old New Milford Road
Brookfield, CT 06804

Art Director: *Nancy Driscoll*
Design Management: *Italiano-Perla Design*

Photographs courtesy of:
John W. McDonough: cover, 3, 25, 31, 37, 38,
41, 46; AP/Wide World Photos: 4, 6, 17, 21, 22, 28, 30,
33, 35, 40, 44; *Lansing State Journal:* 10-11, 15.

Library of Congress Cataloging-in-Publication Data

Gutman, Bill.
Magic Johnson : hero on and off court / by Bill Gutman.
p. cm. — (Millbrook sports world)
Includes bibliographical references (p. 46) and index.
Summary: Examines Magic Johnson's career as a record-
breaking champion with the L.A. Lakers and discusses his
fight against AIDS.
ISBN 1-56294-287-5 (lib. bdg.)
1. Johnson, Earvin, 1959- —Juvenile literature.
2. Basketball players—United States—
Biography—Juvenile literature.
[1. Johnson, Earvin, 1959- . 2. Basketball players.
3. Afro-Americans—Biography.] I. Title. II. Series.
GV884.J63G88 1992
796.323'092—dc20
[B]
92-5002   CIP AC

MAGIC JOHNSON

The opening game of the 1979 National Basketball Association (NBA) season between the Los Angeles Lakers and San Diego Clippers was billed as "the battle of the big men." The Laker center was 7-foot-1 (216-centimeter) Kareem Abdul-Jabbar. The Clippers had 6-foot-11 (211-centimeter) Bill Walton. Both had been outstanding college centers at the University of California at Los Angeles (UCLA) and were champions as pros. The game was on national television with millions of fans across the country glued to their sets.

But there was also another reason for all the opening-day excitement. This was the first pro game for 6-foot-9 (206-centimeter) Earvin Johnson, Jr., the Los Angeles rookie. Johnson, nicknamed "Magic," was the all-American who had led Michigan State University to the NCAA championship the season before. Basketball fans all over the country couldn't wait to see him play in the NBA. For this was no ordinary rookie. He had been a winner wherever he played.

There was even more attention on the rookie when it was learned that Bill Walton was injured and would not play. The game was close from beginning to end. Led by the hot shooting of guard Lloyd Free, San Diego

Even though Magic was only a twenty-year-old NBA rookie in 1979, he played with seasoned veterans right from the start.

was out in front most of the way. But in the closing minutes of the game the Lakers rallied. Magic Johnson was all over the court. He was scoring and setting up teammates with great passes. Finally, Los Angeles trailed by one

A smiling Magic embraces MVP Kareem Abdul-Jabbar after the Lakers won another world championship in 1985. L.A. won five NBA titles during Magic's great career.

point with just seconds left. Magic got the ball to Abdul-Jabbar, who took his trademark shot, a "sky hook" from about 18 feet (5.49 meters) out. The ball dropped through the hoop, and the Lakers had won!

It was only the first game of the year, but you wouldn't know it by watching Magic Johnson. The Laker rookie leaped onto Kareem Abdul-Jabbar and threw his arms around the big guy's neck. He had a grin on his face from ear to ear. His enthusiasm was contagious. The whole Los Angeles team began to dance around. Even Abdul-Jabbar, who usually played the game without changing his expression, cracked a big smile.

Magic was barely 20 years old at the time of his first pro game, but he had scored 26 points. He proved he was ready for the big time. And he brought something else to the NBA: his great smile and the boyish joy he got from playing the game. He was already an inspiration to his team.

The Magic Johnson era had begun.

THE YOUNG EARVIN

Earvin Johnson, Jr., grew up in Lansing, Michigan. He was born there on August 14, 1959, the son of Christine and Earvin Johnson, Sr. Young Earvin was part of a very large family. His father had three children before he married Earvin's mother, then they had seven more together. Earvin, Jr., was the fourth of the last seven. So there were always nine or ten children living under the same roof. It wasn't always easy, but his parents worked very hard to hold their family together.

Lansing, the capital of Michigan, was not a large city. Many of the people who lived there worked in the automobile industry. The streets were not as dangerous for kids as they were in the bigger cities. There wasn't nearly as much crime, drugs, or violence. When kids went out on the streets of Lansing, they mostly played and had fun. Young Earvin played games like kickball and hide-and-seek. He also learned football, baseball, and basketball on the streets.

The Johnsons lived in a small, yellow frame house on Middle Street. It was in a lower middle-class neighborhood where everyone had to work very hard. Earvin Johnson, Sr., had a job with the Fisher Body Corporation. But working one job wasn't enough to support his large family, so he saved some money and bought an old truck. Then he started his own business cleaning up shops and hauling trash. He did that after putting in eight hours at Fisher Body. Young Earvin saw his father work hard for years, and he learned the value of hard work.

His mother also worked very hard. Christine Johnson took care of all her children at home. But when the youngest were old enough, she also got a job. She worked as a school custodian, then came home to cook and clean. Earvin saw how much his mother was willing to do for her family. One day she was sitting at the table with her eyes closed. She was very tired, and Earvin said to her, "Someday I'm going to be somebody so you won't ever have to work again."

Earvin began playing basketball at the Main Street Elementary School. He was already tall for his age when he was in the third grade. The games were kind of wild then, kids running everywhere. By the time he was in the fourth and fifth grades, he began to see that he was a better player than other kids his age. He also believed that nothing was better than winning

When he was in the fifth grade, Earvin learned a hard lesson. His team was going to play another school for the fifth-grade championship. But just a couple of days before the big game, his teacher told him he couldn't play. The reason was that he had not turned in a school assignment.

At first he thought it wasn't fair. He begged his teacher, telling her the game was for the championship.

"I'm sorry, Earvin," she told him. "This is your punishment for not doing your schoolwork."

When he went home and told his mother, she agreed with the teacher. Earvin didn't play, and his team lost. He wasn't going to let that happen again. After that, he always made sure to finish his schoolwork. He did it in elementary school, junior high, high school, and college. Even though basketball was his first love, he knew it was also important to keep up in school.

By the time Earvin went to Dwight Rich Junior High School in the seventh grade he was already 6 feet (183 centimeters) tall. When he left after the ninth grade, he was 6 feet 5 (196 centimeters). It was at Rich Junior High that his name was in the newspaper for the first time. The story said: "Earvin Johnson scored 26 points to lead Rich Junior High to victory."

He was on his way to becoming a star.

HIGH-SCHOOL STAR

Earvin Johnson was becoming a star on the playgrounds as well. Almost all the city kids who played basketball went to the playgrounds. They played there after school, on weekends, and all summer. Playground ball can be rough and very competitive. Earvin remembered that it was important to win.

"The courts were always packed with guys wanting to play," he said. "The only way you could hold the court was to keep winning."

When he was in the ninth grade, Earvin met Dr. Charles Tucker. Tucker was a school psychologist in Lansing. But he was also a fine basketball player who had been a junior-college All-American. He became Earvin's friend after they played a game of one-on-one. He could see how good Earvin was even then and was teaching him things he would have to know to play both college and professional basketball.

After that, whenever Earvin had to make any decisions, he would always talk to his parents and to Charles Tucker. His friendship with Tucker proved to be a very important one for him.

Earvin's father worked so much that he didn't have much time to spend

with his children. But on Sundays, he would watch NBA games on television with his son.

"My father would show me things like a big guard taking a small guard underneath," Earvin remembered. "Or guys running a pick and roll. By the time I started playing, whenever the coach asked if anybody knew how to do a three-man weave or a left-handed lay-up, I was always the first one up."

In the fall of 1974, Earvin began attending Everett High School in Lansing. He joined the basketball team as a tenth grader and began putting on a show. He could dribble well with either hand. He could already dunk the ball and could pass better than anyone. His coach, George Fox, knew he had a winner.

But one of the seniors wasn't passing the ball to Earvin. The two boys

It was at Everett High School in Lansing that Earvin Johnson began attracting national attention for his basketball skills. He first walked through these doors in the fall of 1974. Before he left he led Everett High to the Michigan state championships, acquired his nickname Magic, and had colleges from all over the country knocking at his door.

argued. Before long, racial slurs were being shouted. For maybe the only time in his life, Earvin thought about quitting. But Coach Fox and Charles Tucker managed to settle him down. Tucker told him he was, by far, the best player on the team and some of the others couldn't handle it.

"How would you feel," Tucker asked, "if some young dude came in and just took over the team?"

Then Earvin understood. Pretty soon, he was getting along fine with his new teammates. He didn't try to do it all by himself. And Everett High School was playing winning basketball. In a game against Jackson Parkside High, Earvin just couldn't be stopped. He wound up with 36 points, grabbed 18 rebounds, and had 16 assists.

After the game, a young reporter named Fred Stabley, Jr., walked up to Earvin.

"I want to give you a nickname," Stabley said. "Is that all right?"

Earvin said it was. Stabley paused a minute, then said, "Can I call you 'Magic'"?

For a moment, Earvin wasn't sure. But the more he thought about it, the more he liked the sound. The next day, the story in the *Lansing State Journal* told about the game and its star, Earvin "Magic" Johnson.

THE MAGIC SPREADS

The new nickname caught on fast. His father thought people would expect too much of his son, *Magic*. Did that mean he could perform miracles on the basketball court? Did it mean his team should never lose?

But Magic had a great season. The team finished with a 22-2 record. The second loss, however, was to Dearborn Fordson High in the state quarterfinals. Magic cried after that defeat. He was just 15 years old, and he couldn't bear to lose.

Besides playing at the high school, Magic also began going to the gym at nearby Michigan State University. There he met Terry Furlow, who was then a star for the Spartans, the nickname of the Michigan State team. Furlow liked Magic and always wanted him on his team during pick-up games. Magic learned a lot from the older players, and his game continued to improve.

When Magic reached his senior year at Everett his one goal was to lead his team to the state championship. He also had to decide about the next year. He knew he wanted to play at the college level—the question was where. There were already several well-known colleges that wanted him to play on their team.

Magic was nearly 6 feet 8 (203 centimeters) by this time. He was scoring between 30 and 40 points a game with ease. But he was playing so well that his teammates were just standing around watching him. Coach Fox told him that when he needed his teammates in a big game, they might not be ready. So Magic changed his game right away. He began scoring less and passing the ball to his teammates more. They began playing better. But when the team really needed a basket, Magic took over and got it.

The result was a state championship. Everett won an exciting overtime game in front of a huge crowd at the Chrysler Arena on the University of Michigan campus. Magic and his teammates had achieved their goal. After the season he was named to the high-school All-American team. Now hundreds of colleges were after him.

Magic finally picked five colleges from which to choose. One by one he made his list smaller until it was down to two schools in his home state—the University of Michigan and Michigan State University. Finally, Magic decided to go to Michigan State.

"In a way," he said, "Michigan has a lot more to offer than Michigan State. They are on national television and have had the more successful program the past few years. But I like the underdog school. I've always been the underdog. Every team I've played on wasn't supposed to win. Even when I went to the playgrounds, I always picked the players who wanted to work hard, not necessarily the best ones."

So Earvin Johnson would not be going to a college that was always a basketball power. But he felt he could make a difference.

"I see an NCAA (National Collegiate Athletic Association) championship in Michigan State's future," he told people.

A CHANGED GAME

In the fall of 1977, Earvin Johnson moved up the road to East Lansing and the Michigan State campus. He was a 6-foot-8 (203-centimeter) point guard, which was unusual. Up to that time, almost all point guards were smaller

Even as a student at Michigan State, Magic always made it look easy. Here he puts one in left-handed—not his shooting hand—in a game against Central Michigan during his sophomore season of 1978-1979.

men, from about 5 feet 10 (178 centimeters) to 6 feet 4 (193 centimeters) tall. There were a few who were shorter, and a number who were taller.

A point guard is the player who does most of the ball-handling. He has to run the offense and be able to do different things. Before Magic, there had never been such a tall point guard who could do so many things so well.

Because of that, Earvin Johnson would help to change the game. He was as big or bigger than many college forwards. He could go underneath and rebound, then dribble the length of the court to start a fast break. He was always in control. He could either go to the hoop himself or pass off to a teammate. It was difficult for the defense to stop him. He used his size, strength, and skills to every advantage.

Michigan State already had an outstanding player in 6-foot-7 (201-centimeter) forward Greg Kelser. And there was another outstanding Lansing player coming to Michigan State. He was 6-foot-8 (203-centimeter) center Jay Vincent. Vincent was Magic's old rival from playground and high-school days. So the Spartans would have a promising ball club.

Once the season started it didn't take long for Magic to make his mark. No one thought the Spartans would be a top team so quickly. But after just 13 games, the team had a 12-1 record.

Each night, Magic did the job against good teams and top players. In a game with Minnesota, he had 31 points, 8 rebounds and 4 assists. Against Illinois he scored 17, had 10 assists, 8 rebounds and 4 steals. He scored 19 points against Wichita, adding an amazing 20 rebounds and 9 assists.

Magic drives past Kentucky All-American Jack Givens during the NCAA Mideast Regional final his freshman year. Notice how he protects the ball with his left arm to prevent Givens from going for the steal.

Magic's coach, Jud Heathcote, praised his freshman star for being an unselfish player.

"In Earvin's case, you don't talk only about the points he scores," Heathcote said. "It's the points he produces. He's conscious of scoring himself, but it isn't an obsession with him. He doesn't worry about getting his average every game."

When the regular season ended, the Spartans were Big Ten champions and had a 25-5 record. Magic averaged 17 points a game, but also had 8 rebounds and 7 assists. He was the only freshman in the country to be named to a major All-American team. In the NCAA tournament, Michigan State lost to Kentucky Wildcats in the regional final. They went on to become national champs. But the Spartans had come close.

In 1978-1979, the Spartans won nine of their first ten, losing only to a very good North Carolina team by one point. But then they suddenly lost four of their next six games, all against Big Ten opponents. That dropped the team out of the top ten in the country and made winning the Big Ten again seem almost impossible.

At that point, Coach Heathcote decided to swing Magic back and forth between guard and forward to better use his talents.

"I thought Earvin could destroy people at guard," the coach said. "But I learned he needs the freedom of being able to set up inside and outside."

The change in strategy worked. The team suddenly came to life. Magic still handled the ball most of the time, especially on the fast break. And it was the Michigan State fast break that was killing opponents, leaving them in the dust. Magic ran the break better than anyone. He had great court vision. That meant he knew where everyone was on the court at all times.

Magic worked especially well with Greg Kelser. If Kelser broke to the basket, Magic would lob a quick pass just above the hoop. The ball would get there just as Kelser reached the top of his jump. Kelser would then grab the pass and slam dunk. It was an exciting play, and the fans loved it.

Again the Spartans were in high gear. They won ten straight before losing their final regular season game to Wisconsin. But by overcoming their mid-season slump they tied for the Big Ten title with a 13-5 conference record and finished with an overall mark of 26-6.

In the NCAA tournament they beat Lamar, 95-64, then topped Louisiana State, 87-71. Magic had 24 points and 12 assists in that one. After that, Michigan State topped Notre Dame, 80-68, to win their regional final. Now they were in the Final Four. One of the four remaining teams would be the national champion.

"This is our chance to win it," Magic said. "Kelser is a senior and as for me, I don't know what I'm going to do about the pros. So this is it."

Michigan State's opponent in the semi-final was the University of Pennsylvania. The duo of Johnson and Kelser ran the Quakers off the court in a matter of minutes.

"A little eye contact is all we need," Greg Kelser said of his great court chemistry with Magic. "I know what he's looking for, and he knows what I'm looking for."

The Spartans ran to a 50-17 half-time lead, then cruised to a 101-67 victory. Magic finished the game with 29 points, 10 rebounds and 10 assists. Kelser had 28 points and 9 rebounds. Now the Spartans would meet Indiana State University, led by its own superstar, Larry Bird. Indiana State was unbeaten and the number-one team in the country.

Larry Bird and Magic were the two biggest college stars in the United States. Both were great team players. They did whatever it took to win. Bird was a 6-foot-9 (206-centimeter) forward. He often said that Magic "was more of a passer and I'm more of a scorer."

Coach Heathcote devised a special "match-up" zone to stop Bird. It kept him from getting open for good shots, and it also clogged the passing lanes. Magic and Greg Kelser then started running and took care of the rest. The Spartans led all the way. Indiana State tried to battle back, but Michigan State ran to a 75-64 victory and won the national championship.

Magic topped all scorers with 24 points, followed by Kelser with 19. Bird also had 19, but didn't have a great shooting game. With the victory, Magic

Soon after celebrating winning the 1979 NCAA championship, Magic was faced with the biggest decision of his career—whether or not to go pro.

made good on his promise that Michigan State would win the national championship.

It was no surprise that Magic became a consensus All-American. That meant he was named to every major all-star team. The question now was whether he would stay at Michigan State or turn pro. Good college players were now allowed to join the NBA even before their class graduated.

If Magic chose to go pro, there would be a huge contract waiting for him. He thought about it carefully. He spoke to his parents and his good friend Charles Tucker. He had always studied hard and kept his grades up. Both his father and Dr. Tucker felt he was ready for the pros.

Magic's mom and dad went with their famous son to the NBA draft in New York in June of 1979. To this day, Magic remains very close to his parents.

Finally, Magic came to a decision. He would leave Michigan State and become a professional basketball player.

ROOKIE CHAMPION

The team with the first pick in the draft before the 1979-1980 season was the Los Angeles Lakers. The Lakers were one of the top teams in the league. They had a superstar center in Kareem Abdul-Jabbar. They also had a fine forward in Jamaal Wilkes and a good, young point guard named Norm Nixon. When the Lakers learned of Magic Johnson's decision to turn pro, they quickly made him their number-one choice. He soon signed a contract and would be earning some $500,000 his first year. He wanted to show the Lakers he was worth every penny.

In 1979, the NBA was not in very good shape. There were some great stars in the league, but something was lacking. The players had a "cool" image and didn't show much emotion during games. Attendance was down, and there weren't many games on television. The league needed something new and exciting. Maybe it would be Magic.

In the first game of the year, Kareem Abdul-Jabbar won it with a last-second sky hook and Magic jumped for joy before a national television audience. He had scored 26 points in his pro debut. Over the next several months, he proved over and over again that it wasn't a fluke.

Against Denver, for example, he had 31 points, including eight straight baskets at one point. In another game against Cleveland, Magic had 24 points, 16 rebounds, and 12 assists. He would have double figures in three offensive categories so often that a new term was made for it—the triple double. Magic made the triple-double part of the NBA vocabulary.

"There are some nights when I feel I can do anything," Magic said. "You really have to love the game to play that way. You can't be afraid to let your emotions out in front of 13,000 people."

Even his veteran teammates saw that he was a special kind of rookie. Forward Jim Chones described him this way: "Magic sees angles a lot of guards don't see, and he gives you the ball in the rhythm of your move so you can go right up with it."

Los Angeles finished the season with a 60-22 record. They were Pacific Division champions and had the second-best record in the league. Magic Johnson had a great rookie season. He averaged 18 points a game, as well as 7.3 assists and 7.7 rebounds. That was a very high number of rebounds for a guard. In fact, he was second on the team only to center Abdul-Jabbar.

In the playoffs, Magic and Kareem led the Lakers into the finals against the Philadelphia 76ers, who were led by their superstar, Julius Erving. After four games, the best-of-seven series was tied at two games each. In the fifth game, the Lakers won the battle, but many thought they would lose the war.

Kareem Abdul-Jabbar had sprained an ankle in L.A.'s 108-103 victory. The big center would not be able to play in the sixth game. And if a seventh game were needed, he might not be ready for that one. Laker coach Paul Westhead told Magic that he would be the team's center for game six.

Rookie Johnson goes to the hoop in a game against the Golden State Warriors. It didn't take Magic long to get used to the rugged style of play in the NBA. Even though he was a guard, his great size enabled him to go inside and score against bigger men.

This had never happened before. A 20-year-old rookie point guard was being asked to move to center in the biggest game of the year. That meant he'd have to play against 7-foot (213-centimeter) Caldwell Jones and 6-foot-11 (211-centimeter) Darryl Dawkins. Many felt he couldn't do it.

Not only did Magic do it, he put together one of the greatest games in NBA history. From the opening tap, Magic was all over the court. He scored from both the inside and outside. He rebounded. He threw pinpoint passes from the pivot. His constant movement kept the Philadelphia centers off balance. When the game was over, the Lakers had a 123-107 victory and were world champions!

Magic was simply . . . magic! He scored 42 points, including 14 straight shots from the foul line. He also had 15 rebounds, seven assists, three steals and a blocked shot.

"What position did I play?" he repeated to a question. "Well, I played center, a little forward, some guard. I tried to think up a name for it, but the best I came up with was C-F-G Rover."

He had also inspired his teammates to play better. Jamaal Wilkes scored 37 points, while Michael Cooper had 16. And they had done it without Kareem. After it ended, Magic was named the Most Valuable Player in the playoffs.

The 76ers's Doug Collins said what a lot of people were thinking about Magic: "I knew he was good, but I never realized he was great."

THE LAKERS AND THE CELTICS

Although Magic Johnson was a champion and had led Michigan State to the NCAA title, he was not named college basketball's Player of the Year in 1979. And although he had led the Lakers to the NBA crown, he was not the NBA Rookie of the Year either. Both those awards went to the same player—Larry Bird.

Bird had gone from Indiana State to the Boston Celtics. He, too, had a great rookie year. He led Boston to the best regular-season record in the NBA. Like Magic, Bird played a brilliant overall game. He, too, sometimes seemed to have eyes in the back of his head and almost always came through at crunch time.

The two players had something else in common: Both brought a new kind of enthusiasm to the NBA. They were the most exciting pair of rookies to play in the league in years. Fans flocked to see them in every city where the Lakers or Celtics played.

Magic had a setback his second year. He injured a knee and had to have surgery. Because of that, he missed 45 games. He was back before the play-offs, but the Lakers lost in the first round. That year, Bird and the Celtics were NBA champs. So the two great rookies from 1979-1980 had each won a championship within two years.

At the outset of his third year, Magic signed a fantastic new contract. Dr. Jerry Buss, the team owner, didn't want to take a chance losing him. He signed Magic to a 25-year, $25 million contract. At the time, it was one of the richest in sports. But the Laker owner felt Magic was worth it. Magic's smile was as big as his talent. He was already a spokesman for the game and

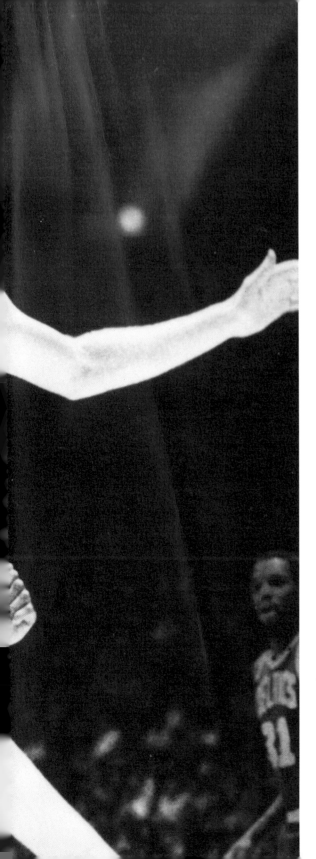

maybe the most popular player in the league.

That same year, 1981-1982, the Lakers had some problems. The players weren't getting along with the coach, Paul Westhead. They felt his style of offense was slowing the team down. After just 11 games, Westhead was dismissed, and Pat Riley became the new coach. He made the Lakers a running, fast-breaking team once again. They were exciting, and they won.

First they won the Pacific Division. Then they rolled into the playoff finals once more. For the second time in three seasons, Los Angeles defeated the Philadelphia 76ers to win the world title. They did it in six games again. In the final game, Magic had 13 points, 13 assists, and 13 rebounds. It was another

Magic and Larry Bird of the Boston Celtics resume their rivalry in the NBA after their epic meeting in the NCAA championship game in 1979. The two great stars are now credited with reviving the popularity of the entire NBA during the decade of the 1980s.

Kareem Abdul-Jabbar and Magic combine to double-team Caldwell Jones.

triple double. Once again he was the playoff MVP.

In 1982-1983, the Lakers made it to the championship round once more, but this time they lost to Philadelphia in four games. Magic led the league in assists and was named to the All-NBA first team for the first time. Then, a year later in 1983-1984, the Lakers finally met the Celtics for the championship.

Magic seemed to be on his way to a new assist record when he dislocated a finger and missed a month. At the All-Star Game he was back in action and set a new record of 22 assists. He also tied Jerry West's Laker Club record of 23 assists in a game and led the league with a 13.1 assist per game average for the year.

He set yet another assist mark in game two of the Western Conference finals. This time he dished out 24 against Phoenix. Then came the finals against the Celtics It was a classic match-up. The Lakers were the speed team that loved to run. The Celtics preferred a

half-court game where players like Bird, forwards Kevin McHale and Cedric Maxwell, center Robert Parish, and guards Dennis Johnson and Danny Ainge could slow things down, work the ball inside, and play rough.

It was a close series. L.A. won the first game, 115-109, upsetting the Celtics at the Boston Garden. They were winning the second, 113-111, with just 15 seconds left. But forward James Worthy made a bad pass, allowing the Celts to tie it. Boston then won it in overtime. Game three in Los Angeles was a 137-104 blowout by the Lakers, with Magic setting a championship series record of 21 assists.

In game four, the Celtics began playing rougher. Boston again won in overtime, 129-125, to even the series at

Magic never had classic form on his jump shot, but it was still an effective offensive weapon that improved throughout his career.

two games each. At one point in that game, the rough play almost ended in a bench-clearing brawl.

"Now we know that if they have to elbow, smack us, or slam us to win, they'll do it," Magic said.

It was 97 humid degrees (36 C) in the old Boston Garden for game five. The heat wore the Lakers down. They were used to playing in the air-conditioned Great Western Forum. The Celtics had been playing in the heat in Boston, and it didn't bother them. They won, 121-103.

Back in L.A. for game six, the Lakers got the running game in gear once again. When their fast break was working well, the Celtics just couldn't run with them. L.A. won it, 119-108, forcing a seventh and final game back at the Boston Garden.

Once again, the Celtics seemed to wear down the Lakers. The difference was on the boards. Boston got 52 rebounds to just 33 for L.A. That stopped the Laker fast break, and the result was a 111-102 Celtics victory. Boston won the championship.

It was not a good series for Magic. Larry Bird averaged 27.4 points a game and was the Most Valuable Player. Magic averaged 18 points a game and set a record with 95 assists. But he also had a record 31 turnovers, losing the ball to the Celtics. Some pointed out that he hadn't made the big play at the end of three of the games.

Magic never worried about his own stats and numbers. The most important stat for him was a "W" for win. But losing was part of the game, too.

In the 1984 championship series against the Celtics,
Magic set a single-game record of 21 assists.

"The series was special," he said. "It's what you play for. I'd rather play in the finals four times and lose than not be in them at all. I'm two and two now, but I can say that I was there."

He was there again in 1984-1985, and he was at his best. Once again it was the Lakers against the Celtics. The Celtics won the first game with very accurate shooting. After that, the Lakers were the better team. With Magic leading the way, they wrapped up the championship with a 111-100 victory in game six. It was Magic's third NBA crown in six years. And this time he had outplayed Larry Bird. In fact, during the regular season Magic had set a record by getting more than 950,000 votes for the All-Star Game. He was becoming the most popular player in basketball.

After the final game against the Celtics, Magic said, "We made 'em lose it. I waited a whole year to get this back. And it's made me stronger. You have to deal with defeat and then see if you can come back."

The rivalry between the Lakers and Celtics was important for another reason. Magic Johnson and Larry Bird were the two biggest stars in the sport. More people watched the championship series between the two teams on television than had ever watched the NBA before. The league was thriving now, and it was Earvin "Magic" Johnson and Larry Bird who had helped bring it back to life.

AN ELDER STATESMAN

In 1984-1985, the same year Magic and Bird were battling for the NBA title a second time, another exciting young player came into the league. He was

Michael Jordan of the Chicago Bulls, an electrifying offensive player who could do it all. His high-flying slam dunks excited fans all over the league. Magic, Bird, and Jordan were the three players who helped the NBA to become even stronger and more popular in the middle and late 1980s.

As for Magic, he just kept working hard at his game. In 1985-1986, he became the first player to get more than one million votes for the All-Star Game. He also led the league in assists for the third time in six years.

In 1986-1987, Magic had his best season. Kareem Abdul-Jabbar turned 40 in April and was slowing down. Magic picked up the slack. He scored, ran the fast break, passed to his teammates, rebounded, and played defense. He averaged a career-best 23.9 points a game and had a career high of 977 total assists.

He was just as good in the playoffs. He led the Lakers into the finals where they defeated the Celtics once again in

Magic flashes his famous trademark smile as NBA Commissioner David Stean presents him with the first of his three MVP awards.

six games. When it was all over, Magic learned he had been named the league's Most Valuable Player for the first time. He was also the playoff MVP for the third time. Earvin "Magic" Johnson was at the top of his game.

In the 1987-1988 season, the Lakers became the first team in nearly 20 years to win two NBA titles in a row. This time L.A. defeated the Detroit Pistons in the final round to take their fifth championship in the 1980s. They were clearly the team of the decade, and it was beginning to look as if Magic Johnson was the player of the decade.

The 1988-1989 season was the last for Kareem Abdul-Jabbar. The big center retired as the NBA's all-time scoring leader. But Magic had another big year and led the Lakers in a sweep of three straight playoff series to reach the finals. Then Magic missed most of the championship series against Detroit with a hamstring injury. The Lakers lost.

After the season, however, Magic was named the league's Most Valuable Player for the second time in three years. He had averaged 22.5 points a game and had another career best with 988 total assists. He also grabbed 607 rebounds, the most he had had since 1983.

Magic was 30 years old for the 1989-1990 season. It was the first time he had played without Kareem Abdul-Jabbar at center. The new Laker center was 7-foot-1 (216-centimeter) Vlade Divac from Yugoslavia. Magic knew it would be a challenge for him to lead the team without Kareem. Now the Lakers weren't expected to win.

Yet they surprised everyone by winning the Pacific Division title with a

Magic concentrates his attention as he gets ready to shoot a free throw. One reason he was so outstanding was his ability to focus on the game night after night.

Magic looks to get the ball to an open teammate during a game with the Houston Rockets.
As a 6-foot-9 (206-centimeter) point guard he could often pass the ball over shorter opponents.

63-19 record. Magic led the team with a 22.3 scoring average, 907 total assists, 132 steals, and 522 rebounds. He was more of a leader than ever— almost a coach—from his point guard spot. For his efforts, he won his third NBA Most Valuable Player Award.

"I had to do different things this year," he said. "My role changed and it was a challenge. For example, without Kareem I started moving inside more. All in all, it has been my most enjoyable time."

But the team lost in the playoffs. The Phoenix Suns topped the Lakers in five games in the conference semi-finals. The Detroit Pistons became NBA champs for a second straight year.

Things continued to change. A year later, in 1990-1991, Mike Dunleavy replaced Pat Riley as the L.A. coach. There were more new players. No longer did the Lakers run, run, run. They were more a half-court team. But their leader was still Earvin Johnson. Magic continued to play the game with skill and a smile.

On the court, he would often talk to the young players. He would tell them where to go, when to cut. With Magic's leadership, the Lakers finished at 58-24. They were five games behind the Portland Trail Blazers in the division race. Magic had his usual great season. On April 15, he became the NBA's all-time assist leader. His 9,888th assist broke the mark set by the great Oscar Robertson.

In the playoffs, Magic led his team in upsets of both the Houston Rockets and the Trail Blazers. Now the Lakers were in the finals against Michael Jordan and the Chicago Bulls. The Bulls were now the running team. Magic and the Lakers tried to slow the game down. They did it in game one, winning on a last second shot by Sam Perkins. But after that it was all Chicago. The Bulls won it in four straight games to become champs.

Magic was quick to compliment Michael Jordan, the man many thought was now the league's greatest star. "Michael is the scariest player in the league," said Magic. "He's been remarkable."

A somber Magic tells the world for the first time that he has contracted the HIV virus and that he would be retiring from the Lakers. His announcement came as a shock to the sports and entertainment worlds.

TRAGEDY STRIKES

Magic was 32 years old when the 1990-1991 season ended. He had always kept himself in top condition and he still loved the game. He looked as if he could play another five years. But when the Lakers opened the 1991-1992 season, Magic wasn't in the lineup. He missed the first three games of the season. At that time, no one really knew why. Then on November 7, 1991, the Lakers called a press conference. A team spokesman said the conference would involve Magic Johnson.

It was Magic himself who stood up and made the announcement that shocked everyone. He said that he was retiring from basketball because he had learned he had the HIV virus.

A virus is a very tiny germ that can cause a disease. The HIV virus causes the disease called AIDS. AIDS stands for Acquired Immune Deficiency Syndrome. A person with AIDS cannot fight off sickness because the immune system—

the body's own way of fighting disease—isn't working properly. So he or she can get many other kinds of diseases just from having AIDS. And people can die from some of these diseases.

Everyone was devastated when Magic Johnson announced he had the HIV virus. But Magic said he was still not sick. It can take from two to ten years for the HIV virus to turn into the AIDS disease.

The doctors, however, wanted Magic to retire from playing basketball right away. They said he could fight the virus better. Professional basketball has a long season. There are 82 regular season games, plus more in the preseason and in the playoffs. It takes a lot of strength to play a whole season. The doctors said Magic could weaken his body by playing. He would need all his strength to fight the HIV virus.

Despite being stricken with the HIV virus, a still-healthy Magic spends as much time on the court as possible.

Magic would miss basketball. It was his first love. But he had married in September 1991 and now had his wife, Cookie, to stand beside him along with the rest of his family. He smiled at the shocked group at the press conference.

"I'm going to beat it," he said. "Life is going to go on for me and I'm going to be a happy man. I guess now I'll get to enjoy some of the other sides of living. But basketball will still be a part of my life."

Magic was ready to face this new challenge. He immediately became a leader in the fight against AIDS and a member of President George Bush's commission on the disease. He has also spoken at many elementary schools and appeared on television warning children about the danger of AIDS. But speaking out for good causes was something he had always done.

Every year, he had run a benefit for the United Negro College Fund. During his career he had raised some $6 million to help educate young black people. He had also set up a program in his hometown of Lansing to help children with reading disabilities. And then, in 1986-1987, Magic was named American Express/NBA Man of the Year for his charity and community work.

Although he didn't play during the first half of the 1991-1992 season, the fans voted Magic to a starting spot for the West in the annual NBA All-Star Game. Magic decided to play and looked like his old self as he scored 25 points in the 153-113 West victory. He was named the game's Most Valuable Player and showed everyone he was still magic out on the court.

There is no doubt that Magic Johnson will always be remembered as a great basketball player. Even though he retired at 32, his career was legendary. And he will always be remembered as a heroic man. He showed everyone how to face tragedy with a brave smile and an upbeat attitude.

Magic looked at the HIV virus the same way he looked at his basketball career. To him, it was another challenge, something he had to work hard at to win. Earvin Johnson had never backed away from a challenge in his life.

MAGIC JOHNSON: HIGHLIGHTS

1959	Born on August 14 in Lansing, Michigan.
1977	Enters Michigan State University. Named to basketball squad.
1978	MSU Spartans are Big Ten basketball champs. Named to All-American college team.
1979	Spartans win NCAA Championship. Named to consensus All-American teams. Signed by NBA Los Angeles Lakers.
1980	Lakers are NBA champions. Named MVP of playoffs.
1982	Lakers are NBA champions. Named MVP of playoffs.
1983	Leads league in assists. Named to All-NBA first team.
1985	Lakers are NBA champions.
1986	Leads league in assists.
1987	Lakers are NBA champions. Named NBA MVP. Named MVP of playoffs.
1988	Lakers are NBA champions.
1989	Named NBA MVP.
1990	Named NBA MVP.
1991	Becomes all-time NBA assist leader with 9,898 assists. Marries Cookie Kelly. Retires from NBA.
1992	Played in All-Star Game on winning team.

FIND OUT MORE

Aaseng, Nathan. *Basketball's Playmakers*. Minneapolis, MN: Lerner, 1983.

Anderson, Dave. *The Story of Basketball*. New York: Morrow Jr. Books, 1988.

Bloom, Marc. *Basketball*. New York: Scholastic, Inc., 1991.

Goodman, Michael E. *Magic Johnson*. New York: Macmillan, 1988.

Gutman, Bill. *Go For It: Basketball*. Lakeville, CT: Grey Castle Press, 1989.

Levin, Rich. *Magic Johnson: Court Magician*. Chicago: Children's Press, 1981.

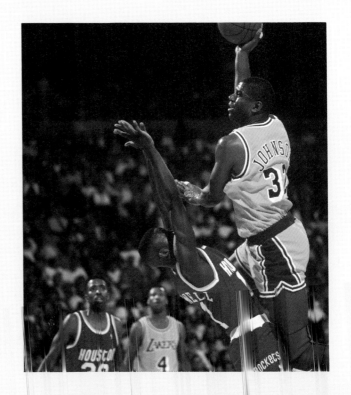

INDEX

Abdul-Jabbar, Kareem, 5, 7, 23, 24, 35, 36, 39
AIDS, 40, 41, 42
Ainge, Danny, 31
All-American
    college, 18
    consensus, 22
    high school, 14
All-NBA, 30
All-Star Game, 30, 42
All-Star Game votes, 34, 35
American Express/NBA Man of the Year, 42
Assist record, 30, 31, 35, 36, 39

Big Ten championship, 18, 19
Bird, Larry, 19, 20, 27, 31, 32, 35
Birth, 7
Boston Celtics, 27, 30, 31, 32, 34, 35
Boston Garden, 31, 32,
Bush, George, 42
Buss, Jerry, 27

"C-F-G Rover", 26
Chicago Bulls, 35, 39
Chones, Jim, 24
Cleveland Cavaliers, 23
Collins, Doug, 26
Cooper, Michael, 26

Dawkins, Darryl, 26
Dearborn Fordson High, 13
Denver Nuggets, 23
Detroit Pistons, 36, 39
Divac, Vlade, 36

Draft, NBA, 23
Dunleavy, Mike, 39
Dwight Rich Junior High School, 9

East Lansing, Michigan, 14
Erving, Julius, 24
Everett High School, 11, 12
    State championship, 13

Fast break, 18, 32
Fisher Body Corporation, 8
Forward, 18
Fox, George, 11, 12, 13
Free, Lloyd, 5
Furlow, Terry, 13

Game average, 26, 29, 32, 35, 38
    freshman year, 18
    NCAA championship, 20
    rookie year, 24
Great Western Forum, 32

Heathcote, Jud, 18, 20
HIV, 40, 43
Houston Rockets, 39

Indiana State University, 19, 20, 27

Jackson Parkside High School, 12
Johnson, Christine, 7, 8
Johnson, Cookie, 42
Johnson, Dennis, 31
Johnson, Earvin, Sr., 7, 8, 11, 12, 22
Jones, Caldwell, 26
Jordan, Michael, 35, 39

Kelser, Greg, 14, 19, 20
Knee injury, 27

Lansing State Journal, 12
Lansing, Michigan, 7, 11, 16, 42
Los Angeles Lakers, 5, 6, 7, 23, 24, 26,
    29, 30, 31, 32, 34, 35, 36, 40
Los Angeles, California, 31, 32

Main Street Elementary School, 8
Match-up zone, 20
Maxwell, Cedric, 31
McHale, Kevin, 31
Michigan State University, 5, 13, 14, 16,
    22, 23, 27
Most Valuable Player
    All-Star Game, 42
    NBA, 36, 38
    NBA championship, 26, 32, 36

National Basketball Association, 5, 11,
    23, 24, 26, 27, 34, 35
    Championship, 26, 27, 29, 30, 32, 34,
    35, 36, 39
    Rookie of the Year, 27
National Collegiate Athletic Association,
    14
    Championship, 5, 20, 22
    Final Four, 19
    Player of the Year, 27
    Title, 27
    Tournament, 18, 19
Nickname ("Magic"), 12
Nixon, Norm, 23

Pacific Division, 29, 38
    Championship, 24
Parish, Robert, 31
Perkins, Sam, 39
Philadelphia 76ers, 24, 26, 29, 30

Phoenix Suns, 30, 39
Playground basketball, 9
Point guard, 14, 16, 18
Portland Trail Blazers, 39
Professional contract, 27

Rebound record, 36
Riley, Pat, 29, 39
Robertson, Oscar, 39

San Diego Clippers, 5
Sky hook, 7
Slam dunk, 35
Spartans (Michigan State), 13, 16, 18, 19,
    20
Stabley, Fred, Jr., 12

Triple Double, 24, 30
Tucker, Charles, 10, 12, 22
Turnover record, 32

UCLA, 5
United Negro College Fund, 42
University of Illinois, 16
University of Michigan, 13, 14
University of Minnesota, 16
University of Pennsylvania, 19
University of Wisconsin, 19

Vincent, Jay, 16

Walton, Bill, 5
West, Jerry, 30
Western Conference, 30
Westhead, Paul, 24, 29
Wilkes, Jamaal, 23 26
Worthy, James, 31

Yugoslavia, 36